This book is primarily a work of fiction. The names, characters, places and incidents are based on the author's imagination. Financial concepts are based on fact and the author's opinion.

First paperback edition 2017

ISBN 978-0-9977910-1-3 (paperback)

Eleven Digital Group, LLC
New York, NY
info@elevendigitalgroup.com

Visit us at www.bullbearkidsbooks.com

Adventures in Finance with Bull & Bear

Borrowing for New Bikes

Created By: Roy & Susan Kim

Illustrated By: Surendhra K. Padayatchi

To Addison and Alexis

Bull and Bear were in the store looking at new bikes.
They were amazed by the selection, but jaws dropped when they saw the price.

A salesman spotted disappointment
and rushed to help them out.
He said, "Please
tell me what
is bothering you...
... so we can flip those
frowns around."

Bear said, "These bikes cost too much. I'm afraid we'll have to leave."

The salesman smiled and said, "I have a deal you won't believe!"

The salesman said that with a loan
they could leave with bikes today.
Bull and Bear were so excited they
didn't know what to say.

Bull and Bear signed papers, then the
salesman said "off you go!"
Because of their excitement, they
forgot to ask, "what's a loan?"

The bikes were used every day...

...for school, work, and of course fun!

They raced around the neighborhood every second there was sun.

Bull liked doing crazy tricks and
jumps all over the place.

Bear liked riding fast and
feeling the wind on her face.

Weeks passed and Bear got a bill. She almost dropped to the floor! Bull came out yelling minutes later...

"DID YOU GET THIS LETTER FROM THE STORE!?"

Bull and Bear owed a lot of money...
...SO MUCH that they were confused.
They were embarrassed and felt lied to. This was not great news.

Bull asked, "Why do we owe so much money?! I mean seriously why so much!"
Bear replied...
"I knew the deal was too good to be true. I also have questions - a bunch!"

Bear did what she should have first
and researched loans on the net.
She learned they borrowed money,
and must repay their debt.

Bear explained, "Loans come with something called interest, so this money is not free. What we owe will keep growing, and could become a problem for you and me."

Bull kicked and screamed and cried out loud - he was very mad. Bear calmly laid out a plan - for this they were both glad.

They paid off part of what they owed, and needed a plan for the rest. Bull shouted, "I have an idea that is absolutely the best!"

Bull explained, "We can put on a live show here in the city...
... and sell lots of tickets
... to friends and family."

Bull continued, "I can use my bike to do tricks for the fans.
Bear... You can manage the money and all the business plans."

Bear didn't like admitting it, but Bull's idea was the best.

They earned enough to pay off their debt. The show was a huge success.

When you come across a deal that seems too good to be true, you are probably right so be careful what you do.

Remember, when you buy something with a loan the money isn't free. It's important when you get a loan you do so responsibly.

About the Creators:

Roy and Susan Kim combined their right and left brains to bring readers educational and entertaining stories about two city kids learning the highs and lows of personal finance. Roy and Susan have witnessed the devastating effects that poor financial decisions can have on families, and they strongly believe that teaching personal finance at a young age will help children become financially secure and stable as adults. Roy grew up in Baltimore, Maryland and studied Finance at the Robert H. Smith School of Business at the University of Maryland, College Park. Roy works with wealth management firms of all sizes that help people around the globe meet their financial goals. Susan is the founder and CEO of Eleven Digital Group, a sales and marketing consulting firm in New York City. Susan brought life to this book series and was instrumental in creating the animated Bull and Bear characters. Roy and Susan moved to New York City from Northern Virginia with their two daughters.

About the Artist:

Surendhra Kumar Padayatchi is a talented artist and illustrator from Tamil Nadu, a rural village in southern India. Surendhra graduated from the Government College of Fine Arts in Chennai, India's oldest art institution established in 1850. Surendhra has been illustrating since 2008, and he is also an author. Surendhra loves drawing, and finds joy and purpose in creating art for our readers to enjoy.

Made in the USA
Monee, IL
05 November 2026

67375661R00017